Sweet Potato Gnocchi Recipes

Delicious and Creative Ways to Make Homemade Sweet Potato Gnocchi

SWEET POTATO GNOCCHI RECIPES

First edition. January 16, 2024.

Copyright © 2024 Sammy Andrews.

ISBN: 979-8224627202

Written by Sammy Andrews.

Table of Contents

Sammy Andrews

Chapter 1: Introduction to Sweet Potato Gnocchi

What is Gnocchi?

Gnocchi, pronounced "nyoh-kee," is a delightful Italian pasta variety known for its small, pillowy dumplings. These little bites are often made with ingredients like potatoes, flour, and eggs, creating a delicate and comforting texture that's beloved by many. While traditional potato gnocchi has been a staple in Italian cuisine for centuries, sweet potato gnocchi offers a unique twist on this classic dish.

Why Sweet Potatoes?

Sweet potatoes are the star of our culinary show, and for good reason. Their natural sweetness, vibrant color, and creamy texture make them an excellent choice for gnocchi. Sweet potato gnocchi provides a delightful balance of sweet and savory flavors, adding depth and complexity to your dishes.

Nutrient-Rich: Sweet potatoes are packed with vitamins, including A and C, as well as fiber and antioxidants, making them a nutritious addition to your meals.

Vibrant Color: The bright orange hue of sweet potatoes not only adds visual appeal to your dishes but also hints at the rich, earthy flavors within.

Versatility: Sweet potatoes can seamlessly transition between sweet and savory preparations, making them an ideal choice for a wide range of recipes.

Essential Ingredients and Tools

Before you embark on your sweet potato gnocchi journey, it's essential to gather the following ingredients and tools:

Ingredients:

- Sweet Potatoes: Look for firm, fresh sweet potatoes with vibrant orange flesh. You'll need about 2 pounds for most recipes.

- All-Purpose Flour: This will help bind the gnocchi together. You may also explore gluten-free alternatives like rice flour for those with dietary restrictions.

- Salt: Essential for seasoning the dough and boiling water.

- Optional Additions: Depending on your recipe, you might use eggs, herbs, or spices to enhance the flavor of your sweet potato gnocchi.

Tools:

- Potato Masher or Ricer: To mash or rice the sweet potatoes until they're smooth and free of lumps.

- Large Mixing Bowl: For combining the sweet potato puree and flour.

- Bench Scraper or Knife: Helpful for cutting the gnocchi into bite-sized pieces.

- Fork or Gnocchi Board: To create the characteristic ridges on the gnocchi, which help hold onto sauces.

- Large Pot: For boiling the gnocchi.

- Slotted Spoon: To gently lift the cooked gnocchi out of the boiling water.

- Skillet or Saucepan: For sautéing or simmering your chosen sauces.

Sweet potato gnocchi is a versatile and delectable addition to your culinary repertoire. In the following chapters, we'll explore a wide array of recipes, from classic preparations to innovative creations, so you can savor the delicious possibilities of this delightful dish. Whether you're a seasoned chef or a beginner in the kitchen, you'll find something to love in these pages. Let's start cooking!

Chapter 2: Classic Sweet Potato Gnocchi

In this chapter, we'll dive into the heart of sweet potato gnocchi preparation by exploring the classic recipe that has delighted generations. Before we get started, let's take a moment to appreciate the distinction between traditional potato gnocchi and our sweet potato version.

Traditional Potato Gnocchi vs. Sweet Potato Gnocchi

Traditional Potato Gnocchi:

Traditional potato gnocchi, often made with russet or Yukon Gold potatoes, has a long history in Italian cuisine. These gnocchi are known for their light, fluffy texture and mild potato flavor. They pair wonderfully with a variety of sauces, from simple tomato and basil to creamy Alfredo.

Sweet Potato Gnocchi:

Sweet potato gnocchi, on the other hand, bring a unique twist to the table. The addition of sweet potatoes infuses these dumplings with a hint of sweetness and a vibrant orange color. This variation introduces a delightful contrast to traditional potato gnocchi and pairs exceptionally well with both savory and sweet sauces. Whether you prefer classic or sweet potato, both options have their own charm.

Step-by-Step Recipe

Now, let's roll up our sleeves and create our classic sweet potato gnocchi from scratch. Here's a step-by-step guide to get you started:

Ingredients:

- 2 pounds of sweet potatoes (about 3 medium-sized sweet potatoes)
- 2 cups of all-purpose flour, plus extra for dusting
- 1 teaspoon of salt

Instructions:

1. Prepare the Sweet Potatoes: Start by preheating your oven to 400°F (200°C). Pierce the sweet potatoes several times with a fork and place them on a baking sheet. Bake for about 45 minutes to 1 hour, or until they're tender and easily pierced with a fork.
2. Cool and Peel: Allow the sweet potatoes to cool slightly, then peel off the skin. Mash them thoroughly using a potato masher or a potato ricer until you have smooth, lump-free sweet potato puree.
3. Add Flour and Salt: In a large mixing bowl, combine the sweet potato puree, 2 cups of all-purpose flour, and 1 teaspoon of salt. Mix until the ingredients come together to form a soft dough.
4. Knead the Dough: Turn the dough out onto a lightly floured surface. Knead it gently, adding more flour as needed to prevent sticking, until you have a smooth, pliable dough.
5. Divide and Roll: Divide the dough into small portions. Roll each portion into a long rope, about 1/2 inch in diameter.
6. Cut into Pieces: Use a sharp knife or a bench scraper to cut the ropes into bite-sized pieces, approximately 1 inch each. Optionally, you can create the traditional gnocchi ridges by gently pressing each piece with a fork or a gnocchi board.

7. Cook the Gnocchi: Bring a large pot of salted water to a boil. Carefully add the gnocchi to the boiling water and cook until they float to the surface, which usually takes about 2-3 minutes.

8. Serve: Once the gnocchi float, remove them with a slotted spoon and transfer them to your preferred sauce. Classic choices include sage and brown butter, marinara, or a simple olive oil and garlic sauce. Garnish with grated Parmesan cheese and fresh herbs, if desired.

Serving Suggestions

Classic sweet potato gnocchi are incredibly versatile and pair wonderfully with a variety of sauces and accompaniments. Here are some serving suggestions to get you started:

Sage and Brown Butter: Drizzle your gnocchi with a rich and nutty sage brown butter sauce for a classic Italian flavor.

Marinara Sauce: Toss your gnocchi in a vibrant tomato marinara sauce and top with fresh basil and grated Parmesan.

Pesto: Sweet potato gnocchi's natural sweetness pairs beautifully with fresh basil pesto and pine nuts.

Creamy Alfredo: For a luxurious twist, serve your gnocchi with a creamy Alfredo sauce and a sprinkle of grated Parmesan.

Roasted Vegetables: Create a hearty dish by adding roasted vegetables like asparagus, cherry tomatoes, or Brussels sprouts to your gnocchi.

Fresh Herbs: Garnish with chopped fresh herbs such as basil, parsley, or chives for a burst of flavor.

Now that you've mastered the classic sweet potato gnocchi recipe and learned some delicious serving options, you're well on your way to creating delightful meals that will impress family and friends. In the following chapters, we'll explore various sweet potato gnocchi variations and sauces, so you can continue to expand your culinary horizons.

Chapter 3: Sweet Potato Gnocchi Variations

In this chapter, we'll explore exciting variations of sweet potato gnocchi that will add a burst of flavor and creativity to your culinary repertoire. Whether you're looking to infuse more vegetables or explore gluten-free options, there's a sweet potato gnocchi variation for everyone.

Spinach and Sweet Potato Gnocchi

Spinach and sweet potato gnocchi combine the earthy sweetness of sweet potatoes with the vibrant green goodness of spinach. This variation not only adds a lovely green hue to your gnocchi but also introduces a subtle, vegetal flavor that pairs beautifully with various sauces.

Ingredients:

- 2 pounds of sweet potatoes (about 3 medium-sized sweet potatoes)
- 2 cups of fresh spinach, blanched and finely chopped
- 2 cups of all-purpose flour, plus extra for dusting
- 1 teaspoon of salt

Instructions:

1. Prepare the Sweet Potatoes: Follow the same steps for baking and mashing sweet potatoes as outlined in the classic sweet potato gnocchi recipe (Chapter 2).
2. Add Spinach: Blanch the fresh spinach by briefly immersing it in boiling water, then immediately plunging it into ice water. Drain and finely chop the blanched spinach. Mix it into the sweet potato puree before adding flour and salt.
3. Continue with the Classic Recipe: Proceed with the classic sweet potato gnocchi recipe (Chapter 2) by adding flour and salt, kneading the dough, and shaping the gnocchi. Cooking

and serving instructions remain the same.

Butternut Squash and Sweet Potato Gnocchi

Butternut squash and sweet potato gnocchi is a delightful twist on the classic recipe. The combination of these two sweet and creamy ingredients results in gnocchi with a rich, autumnal flavor that's perfect for fall and winter meals.

Ingredients:

- 1 pound of sweet potatoes (about 2 medium-sized sweet potatoes)
- 1 pound of butternut squash
- 2 cups of all-purpose flour, plus extra for dusting
- 1 teaspoon of salt

Instructions:

1. Prepare the Sweet Potatoes and Butternut Squash: Peel and dice the butternut squash into small cubes. Follow the same steps for baking and mashing sweet potatoes as outlined in the classic sweet potato gnocchi recipe (Chapter 2).
2. Combine Sweet Potatoes and Butternut Squash: Mix the mashed sweet potatoes and mashed butternut squash together in a large bowl before adding flour and salt.
3. Continue with the Classic Recipe: Proceed with the classic sweet potato gnocchi recipe (Chapter 2) by adding flour and salt, kneading the dough, and shaping the gnocchi. Cooking and serving instructions remain the same.

Gluten-Free Options

For those with dietary restrictions or seeking gluten-free alternatives, you can still enjoy the deliciousness of sweet potato gnocchi by using gluten-free flours such as rice flour, almond flour, or a gluten-free flour blend. Simply substitute the all-purpose flour in the classic sweet potato gnocchi recipe (Chapter 2) with your preferred gluten-free flour in a 1:1 ratio.

Experiment with different gluten-free flours to find your favorite texture and flavor. You'll be amazed at how versatile sweet potato gnocchi can be, even when adhering to specific dietary needs.

With these sweet potato gnocchi variations, you can elevate your cooking game and introduce exciting flavors to your meals. Feel free to mix and match these variations with the delicious sauces and serving suggestions from Chapter 2 to create endless mouthwatering possibilities.

Chapter 4: Flavored Sweet Potato Gnocchi

In this chapter, we'll explore the world of flavored sweet potato gnocchi, where each bite bursts with unique and enticing tastes. These variations add a gourmet touch to your sweet potato gnocchi, making them perfect for special occasions or when you simply want to indulge in something extraordinary.

Sage and Brown Butter Sweet Potato Gnocchi

Sage and brown butter is a classic Italian flavor combination that pairs exceptionally well with sweet potato gnocchi. The nutty richness of brown butter and the earthy aroma of sage create a harmonious sauce that complements the natural sweetness of the gnocchi.

Ingredients:

- 1 batch of sweet potato gnocchi (classic or your preferred variation)
- 1/2 cup (1 stick) of unsalted butter
- A handful of fresh sage leaves
- Salt and freshly ground black pepper, to taste
- Grated Parmesan cheese (optional, for serving)

Instructions:

1. Cook the Gnocchi: Prepare your sweet potato gnocchi as outlined in the classic sweet potato gnocchi recipe (Chapter 2) or your chosen variation.
2. Make the Sage Brown Butter: In a large skillet, melt the unsalted butter over medium heat. Add the fresh sage leaves and cook until the butter turns a beautiful golden brown color and the sage leaves become crispy. Be sure to keep an eye on it, as brown butter can go from perfect to burnt quickly.

3. Combine with Gnocchi: Once your gnocchi are cooked and drained, transfer them to the skillet with the sage brown butter. Toss gently to coat the gnocchi evenly in the flavorful sauce. Season with salt and freshly ground black pepper to taste.

4. Serve: Plate your sage and brown butter sweet potato gnocchi, garnish with additional crispy sage leaves, and sprinkle with grated Parmesan cheese if desired. Enjoy this delightful, aromatic dish!

Roasted Garlic and Parmesan Sweet Potato Gnocchi

Roasted garlic and Parmesan elevate sweet potato gnocchi to a whole new level of savory goodness. The roasted garlic adds a mellow, caramelized sweetness, while the Parmesan cheese brings a salty, umami richness to the dish.

Ingredients:

- 1 batch of sweet potato gnocchi (classic or your preferred variation)
- 1 whole bulb of garlic
- 2 tablespoons of olive oil
- 1/2 cup of grated Parmesan cheese
- Salt and freshly ground black pepper, to taste
- Chopped fresh parsley (optional, for garnish)

Instructions:

1. Roast the Garlic: Preheat your oven to 400°F (200°C). Cut off the top of the garlic bulb to expose the cloves, drizzle it with olive oil, and wrap it in aluminum foil. Roast in the oven for about 30-35 minutes, or until the garlic cloves are soft and golden brown.
2. Prepare the Gnocchi: Cook your sweet potato gnocchi as outlined in the classic sweet potato gnocchi recipe (Chapter 2) or your chosen variation.
3. Mash the Roasted Garlic: Squeeze the roasted garlic cloves out of their skins into a small bowl. Mash them into a paste with a fork.
4. Combine with Gnocchi: In a large bowl, mix the roasted garlic paste with the cooked gnocchi. Add grated Parmesan cheese and toss to combine. Season with salt and freshly ground black pepper to taste.
5. Serve: Plate your roasted garlic and Parmesan sweet potato

gnocchi, garnish with chopped fresh parsley if desired, and savor the delightful, savory flavors.

Herbed Sweet Potato Gnocchi

Herbed sweet potato gnocchi offer a burst of fresh, fragrant flavors. By incorporating various herbs into your gnocchi dough, you can create a dish that's not only delicious but also visually appealing.

Ingredients:

- 1 batch of sweet potato gnocchi (classic or your preferred variation)
- A combination of fresh herbs (such as basil, parsley, and chives), finely chopped
- Olive oil
- Salt and freshly ground black pepper, to taste
- Grated Parmesan cheese (optional, for serving)

Instructions:

1. Prepare the Gnocchi: Cook your sweet potato gnocchi as outlined in the classic sweet potato gnocchi recipe (Chapter 2) or your chosen variation.
2. Toss with Herbs: In a large bowl, toss the cooked gnocchi with a generous drizzle of olive oil and your finely chopped fresh herbs. Be creative with your herb selection to customize the flavors to your liking.
3. Season and Serve: Season your herbed sweet potato gnocchi with salt and freshly ground black pepper to taste. Serve as is or sprinkle with grated Parmesan cheese for an added layer of flavor.

These flavored sweet potato gnocchi recipes showcase the culinary possibilities of this delightful dish. Experiment with different herbs and ingredients to create your own unique flavor combinations, and impress your family and friends with gourmet sweet potato gnocchi dishes.

Chapter 5: Sweet Potato Gnocchi Sauces

In this chapter, we'll explore a trio of delectable sauces that perfectly complement the sweet and tender pillows of sweet potato gnocchi. Whether you're in the mood for a classic tomato-based sauce, a creamy indulgence, or the vibrant flavors of pesto, we've got you covered.

Classic Marinara Sauce

Marinara sauce is a timeless and versatile choice for dressing your sweet potato gnocchi. Its robust tomato flavor, accented with aromatic herbs, provides a delightful contrast to the natural sweetness of the gnocchi.

Ingredients:

- 2 tablespoons of olive oil
- 1 small onion, finely chopped
- 3 cloves of garlic, minced
- 1 (28-ounce) can of crushed tomatoes
- 1 teaspoon of dried basil
- 1 teaspoon of dried oregano
- 1/2 teaspoon of sugar (optional, to balance acidity)
- Salt and freshly ground black pepper, to taste
- Fresh basil leaves, for garnish
- Grated Parmesan cheese, for serving (optional)

Instructions:

1. Sauté the Aromatics: In a saucepan, heat the olive oil over medium heat. Add the finely chopped onion and sauté until translucent, about 3-4 minutes. Add the minced garlic and sauté for another minute until fragrant.
2. Simmer the Sauce: Pour in the crushed tomatoes, dried basil,

dried oregano, and sugar (if using). Season with salt and freshly ground black pepper to taste. Bring the sauce to a gentle simmer, then reduce the heat and let it simmer for about 15-20 minutes, stirring occasionally. This allows the flavors to meld and the sauce to thicken.

3. Serve: Pour the marinara sauce over your cooked sweet potato gnocchi, garnish with fresh basil leaves, and sprinkle with grated Parmesan cheese if desired. It's a classic pairing that's hard to resist.

Creamy Alfredo Sauce

Indulge in the velvety richness of creamy Alfredo sauce, which provides a luscious contrast to the sweetness of sweet potato gnocchi. This sauce is comfort food at its finest.

Ingredients:

- 1/2 cup (1 stick) of unsalted butter
- 1 cup of heavy cream
- 1 cup of grated Parmesan cheese
- Salt and freshly ground black pepper, to taste
- Fresh parsley, for garnish

Instructions:

1. Melt the Butter: In a saucepan over medium heat, melt the unsalted butter. Once melted, add the heavy cream, stirring constantly until well combined.
2. Add Parmesan Cheese: Gradually add the grated Parmesan cheese to the sauce, continuing to stir until it's fully melted and the sauce becomes creamy and smooth. Season with salt and freshly ground black pepper to taste.
3. Serve: Pour the creamy Alfredo sauce over your cooked sweet potato gnocchi, garnish with fresh parsley, and savor the luxuriousness of this decadent pairing.

Pesto and Walnut Sauce

For a burst of fresh, vibrant flavors, look no further than pesto and walnut sauce. The basil, garlic, and nutty notes of this sauce perfectly complement the sweet potato gnocchi.

Ingredients:

- 2 cups of fresh basil leaves
- 2 cloves of garlic
- 1/2 cup of toasted walnuts
- 1/2 cup of grated Parmesan cheese
- 1/2 cup of extra-virgin olive oil
- Salt and freshly ground black pepper, to taste
- Grated Parmesan cheese, for serving (optional)

Instructions:

1. Prepare the Pesto: In a food processor, combine the fresh basil leaves, garlic cloves, toasted walnuts, and grated Parmesan cheese. Pulse until everything is finely chopped.
2. Blend with Olive Oil: With the food processor running, slowly drizzle in the extra-virgin olive oil until the mixture becomes a smooth, vibrant pesto sauce. Season with salt and freshly ground black pepper to taste.
3. Serve: Toss your cooked sweet potato gnocchi in the pesto and walnut sauce, ensuring they're well coated. For an extra layer of flavor, sprinkle with grated Parmesan cheese before serving.

These sweet potato gnocchi sauces provide a spectrum of flavors to elevate your dining experience. Mix and match them with your favorite gnocchi variations from earlier chapters, and don't hesitate to experiment with additional ingredients to make them your own.

Chapter 6: Gourmet Sweet Potato Gnocchi

In this chapter, we'll delve into the world of gourmet sweet potato gnocchi, where luxurious ingredients and complex flavors take center stage. These gourmet recipes are perfect for special occasions or when you want to treat yourself to an exceptional dining experience.

Lobster and Sweet Potato Gnocchi

Sweet potato gnocchi take on a new level of opulence when paired with succulent lobster. This gourmet dish combines the natural sweetness of the gnocchi with the delicate flavor of lobster and a rich, creamy sauce.

Ingredients:

- 1 batch of sweet potato gnocchi (classic or your preferred variation)
- 2 lobster tails, cooked and meat removed
- 2 tablespoons of unsalted butter
- 2 cloves of garlic, minced
- 1/2 cup of heavy cream
- 1/4 cup of dry white wine
- Salt and freshly ground black pepper, to taste
- Chopped fresh chives, for garnish

Instructions:

1. Prepare the Gnocchi: Cook your sweet potato gnocchi as outlined in the classic sweet potato gnocchi recipe (Chapter 2) or your chosen variation.
2. Cook the Lobster: In a large skillet, melt the unsalted butter over medium heat. Add the minced garlic and cook for about 30 seconds until fragrant. Add the cooked lobster meat and

sauté briefly to warm it.

3. Add Cream and Wine: Pour in the heavy cream and dry white wine. Bring the mixture to a gentle simmer, stirring occasionally. Let it simmer for about 2-3 minutes until the sauce thickens slightly. Season with salt and freshly ground black pepper to taste.

4. Combine with Gnocchi: Toss the cooked sweet potato gnocchi in the lobster and cream sauce, ensuring they are well coated.

5. Serve: Plate your lobster and sweet potato gnocchi, garnish with chopped fresh chives, and savor this decadent gourmet delight.

Truffle and Mushroom Sweet Potato Gnocchi

Truffle and mushroom sweet potato gnocchi offer an earthy and luxurious flavor profile that's perfect for truffle lovers. The delicate sweetness of the gnocchi pairs beautifully with the deep, umami notes of truffle and mushrooms.

Ingredients:

- 1 batch of sweet potato gnocchi (classic or your preferred variation)
- 1 cup of mixed mushrooms (such as cremini, shiitake, or porcini), sliced
- 2 tablespoons of truffle oil
- 2 tablespoons of unsalted butter
- 2 cloves of garlic, minced
- Salt and freshly ground black pepper, to taste
- Grated Parmesan cheese, for serving (optional)
- Fresh parsley, for garnish

Instructions:

1. Prepare the Gnocchi: Cook your sweet potato gnocchi as outlined in the classic sweet potato gnocchi recipe (Chapter 2) or your chosen variation.
2. Sauté the Mushrooms: In a large skillet, heat the truffle oil and unsalted butter over medium heat. Add the minced garlic and sauté for about 30 seconds until fragrant. Add the sliced mushrooms and cook until they are tender and browned, about 5-7 minutes. Season with salt and freshly ground black pepper to taste.
3. Combine with Gnocchi: Toss the cooked sweet potato gnocchi in the sautéed mushroom and truffle mixture, ensuring they are well coated.
4. Serve: Plate your truffle and mushroom sweet potato gnocchi,

garnish with grated Parmesan cheese (if desired), and sprinkle with fresh parsley for an added burst of flavor.

Blue Cheese and Walnut Sweet Potato Gnocchi

Blue cheese and walnut sweet potato gnocchi offer a bold and satisfying flavor combination. The creamy, tangy notes of blue cheese and the nutty crunch of walnuts create a memorable gourmet experience.

Ingredients:

- 1 batch of sweet potato gnocchi (classic or your preferred variation)
- 1/2 cup of crumbled blue cheese
- 1/2 cup of toasted walnuts, chopped
- 2 tablespoons of unsalted butter
- Salt and freshly ground black pepper, to taste
- Chopped fresh chives, for garnish

Instructions:

1. Prepare the Gnocchi: Cook your sweet potato gnocchi as outlined in the classic sweet potato gnocchi recipe (Chapter 2) or your chosen variation.
2. Create the Sauce: In a large skillet, melt the unsalted butter over medium heat. Add the crumbled blue cheese and toasted walnuts. Stir until the blue cheese starts to melt and the walnuts are coated.
3. Combine with Gnocchi: Toss the cooked sweet potato gnocchi in the blue cheese and walnut sauce, ensuring they are well coated
4. Serve: Plate your blue cheese and walnut sweet potato gnocchi, garnish with chopped fresh chives, and enjoy the bold, gourmet flavors of this dish.

These gourmet sweet potato gnocchi recipes are sure to impress even the most discerning palates. Experiment with these luxurious ingredients to create memorable meals for special occasions or when you simply want to treat yourself to something extraordinary.

Chapter 7: Sweet Potato Gnocchi for Kids

In this chapter, we'll explore kid-friendly versions of sweet potato gnocchi that will not only delight young taste buds but also make mealtime more enjoyable for the entire family. We'll focus on recipes that are not only tasty but also fun and nutritious.

Kid-Friendly Recipes

Introducing children to the joys of sweet potato gnocchi can be an exciting culinary adventure. These recipes are designed to appeal to kids' palates and make them eager to try new flavors.

1. Cheesy Sweet Potato Gnocchi:

Ingredients: Sweet potato gnocchi, cheese sauce (a simple blend of milk, cheddar cheese, and a pinch of nutmeg)

Instructions: Toss cooked sweet potato gnocchi in a creamy cheese sauce for a comforting and familiar dish that kids love.

2. Mini Meatball Sweet Potato Gnocchi:

Ingredients: Sweet potato gnocchi, mini meatballs (made with ground beef or turkey, breadcrumbs, egg, and seasoning), tomato sauce

Instructions: Combine sweet potato gnocchi with mini meatballs and a flavorful tomato sauce for a kid-friendly twist on spaghetti and meatballs.

3. Sweet Potato Gnocchi and Mini Sausages:

Ingredients: Sweet potato gnocchi, mini sausages (sliced), a simple tomato-based sauce

Instructions: Create a fun and hearty dish by pairing sweet potato gnocchi with bite-sized sausages in a flavorful tomato sauce.

Fun Shapes and Colors

Make mealtime exciting by shaping sweet potato gnocchi into fun forms and adding vibrant colors that capture kids' imaginations.

1. Animal Shapes:

Use sweet potato gnocchi dough to create animal-shaped gnocchi using cookie cutters or molds. Let kids choose their favorite animals and get creative in the kitchen.

2. Rainbow Gnocchi:

Divide the gnocchi dough into portions and add natural food colorings (such as beet juice for red, spinach for green, or carrot puree for orange) to create a rainbow of colorful gnocchi.

3. Alphabet Gnocchi:

Form the sweet potato gnocchi into letters of the alphabet, allowing kids to spell out words or simply have fun with their food.

Sneaky Veggie Gnocchi

Getting kids to eat their vegetables can be a challenge, but these sneaky veggie gnocchi recipes hide nutritious ingredients in delicious packages.

1. Sweet Potato and Spinach Gnocchi:

Ingredients: Sweet potato gnocchi, fresh spinach puree

Instructions: Mix fresh spinach puree into the gnocchi dough to create vibrant green gnocchi with added nutrients.

2. Carrot and Sweet Potato Gnocchi:

Ingredients: Sweet potato gnocchi, carrot puree

Instructions: Incorporate carrot puree into the gnocchi dough for an appealing orange hue and a dose of vitamin A.

3. Beetroot and Sweet Potato Gnocchi:

Ingredients: Sweet potato gnocchi, beetroot puree

Instructions: Add beetroot puree to the gnocchi dough for a striking magenta color and a boost of antioxidants.

These kid-friendly sweet potato gnocchi recipes aim to make mealtime enjoyable and nutritious for children while introducing them to the wonderful world of flavors. Encourage them to get involved in the cooking process and have fun with their food.

Chapter 8: Sweet Potato Gnocchi for Entertaining

In this chapter, we'll explore how sweet potato gnocchi can take center stage at your dinner parties and gatherings. From impressive dishes that will wow your guests to make-ahead tips and the art of plating and presentation, you'll be the host or hostess with the mostest.

Impressive Dinner Party Dishes

When entertaining guests, you want to serve dishes that not only taste exceptional but also leave a lasting impression. These sweet potato gnocchi recipes are perfect for making your dinner parties unforgettable.

1. Lobster and Sweet Potato Gnocchi with Champagne Cream Sauce:

Ingredients: Sweet potato gnocchi, lobster meat, champagne, heavy cream, shallots, chives, butter

Instructions: Create an elegant dish by pairing sweet potato gnocchi with succulent lobster and a luxurious champagne cream sauce. Garnish with fresh chives for a touch of sophistication.

2. Truffle and Mushroom Sweet Potato Gnocchi with Parmesan Crisps:

Ingredients: Sweet potato gnocchi, mixed mushrooms, truffle oil, heavy cream, Parmesan cheese, thyme

Instructions: Impress your guests with the earthy flavors of truffle and mushrooms, combined with sweet potato gnocchi. Serve alongside delicate Parmesan crisps for added texture and flavor.

3. Blue Cheese and Walnut Sweet Potato Gnocchi with Pear and Arugula Salad:

Ingredients: Sweet potato gnocchi, blue cheese sauce, toasted walnuts, fresh pears, arugula, honey

Instructions: Create a sophisticated sweet and savory dish by pairing sweet potato gnocchi with a rich blue cheese and walnut sauce, complemented by a refreshing pear and arugula salad drizzled with honey.

Make-Ahead Tips

Hosting a dinner party can be less stressful with proper planning. Here are some make-ahead tips to ensure your sweet potato gnocchi dishes come together smoothly:

1. Prepare the Gnocchi in Advance:

You can make the sweet potato gnocchi ahead of time and freeze them on a baking sheet. Once frozen, transfer them to a resealable bag or airtight container. When guests arrive, you can cook them directly from the freezer.

2. Sauces and Components:

Prepare sauces, garnishes, and accompaniments in advance. Store them in separate containers and refrigerate. Reheat sauces gently before serving.

3. Timing is Key:

Plan your cooking schedule, so you have enough time to focus on plating and presentation when your guests arrive. Timing is crucial for serving hot and delicious sweet potato gnocchi.

Plating and Presentation

The art of plating and presentation can elevate your sweet potato gnocchi dishes from ordinary to extraordinary. Here are some tips to make your dishes visually stunning:

1. Plate with Precision:

Use serving utensils and molds to arrange sweet potato gnocchi neatly on each plate. Pay attention to spacing and alignment for an elegant look.

2. Garnish with Flair:

Add a final touch by garnishing your dishes with fresh herbs, microgreens, edible flowers, or grated cheese. These small details make a big difference.

3. Color Contrast:

Consider the colors of your ingredients and how they complement each other. For example, a drizzle of colorful sauce over golden sweet potato gnocchi can create a striking visual contrast.

4. Serve on Beautiful Tableware:

Choose elegant dishes and tableware that complement the aesthetics of your dishes. Well-chosen table settings can enhance the dining experience.

Impress your guests not only with the incredible flavors of your sweet potato gnocchi creations but also with their stunning presentation. With these entertaining tips, your dinner parties will be memorable occasions filled with gourmet delights.

Chapter 9: Sweet Potato Gnocchi Bowls

In this chapter, we'll explore the versatile world of sweet potato gnocchi bowls. These bowls are not only delicious but also customizable, allowing you to create a variety of balanced and satisfying meals.

Buddha Bowl with Sweet Potato Gnocchi

A Buddha bowl is a colorful and nutritious dish that typically consists of a variety of vegetables, grains, and proteins. Adding sweet potato gnocchi to the mix brings a unique twist to this health-conscious meal.

Ingredients:

- 1 batch of sweet potato gnocchi (classic or your preferred variation)
- Assorted roasted vegetables (such as bell peppers, broccoli, carrots, and zucchini)
- Cooked quinoa or brown rice
- Chickpeas, roasted or sautéed
- Fresh greens (spinach, kale, or arugula)
- Avocado slices
- Hummus or tahini sauce for drizzling
- Sprouts or microgreens for garnish
- Salt and pepper, to taste

Instructions:

1. Prepare the Gnocchi: Cook your sweet potato gnocchi as outlined in the classic sweet potato gnocchi recipe (Chapter 2) or your chosen variation.

2. Assemble the Bowl: Start with a base of cooked quinoa or brown rice. Arrange the cooked sweet potato gnocchi, roasted vegetables, chickpeas, fresh greens, and avocado slices in separate sections of the bowl.

3. Drizzle and Garnish: Drizzle your choice of hummus or tahini sauce over the bowl. Sprinkle with sprouts or microgreens for a burst of freshness. Season with salt and pepper to taste.

4. Customize: Feel free to customize your Buddha bowl with your favorite vegetables, proteins, and sauces. The sweet potato gnocchi will add a delightful touch to this balanced meal.

Mediterranean Gnocchi Bowl

Capture the flavors of the Mediterranean in a satisfying gnocchi bowl that combines sweet potato gnocchi with Mediterranean-inspired ingredients.

Ingredients:

- 1 batch of sweet potato gnocchi (classic or your preferred variation)
- Cherry tomatoes, halved
- Cucumber, diced
- Kalamata olives, pitted and sliced
- Red onion, thinly sliced
- Feta cheese, crumbled
- Fresh basil leaves, torn
- Extra-virgin olive oil
- Balsamic glaze
- Salt and pepper, to taste

Instructions:

1. Prepare the Gnocchi: Cook your sweet potato gnocchi as outlined in the classic sweet potato gnocchi recipe (Chapter 2) or your chosen variation.
2. Assemble the Bowl: In a bowl or on a plate, arrange the cooked sweet potato gnocchi alongside the cherry tomatoes, cucumber, Kalamata olives, red onion, and crumbled feta cheese.
3. Garnish: Scatter torn basil leaves over the bowl. Drizzle with extra-virgin olive oil and balsamic glaze for a burst of Mediterranean flavors. Season with salt and pepper to taste.
4. Serve: Enjoy this Mediterranean-inspired gnocchi bowl as a fresh and satisfying meal that celebrates the essence of the Mediterranean cuisine.

Breakfast Gnocchi Bowl

Who says sweet potato gnocchi is just for dinner? This breakfast gnocchi bowl is a delightful way to kickstart your day with a twist on a classic breakfast.

Ingredients:

- 1 batch of sweet potato gnocchi (classic or your preferred variation)
- Scrambled eggs or tofu scramble for a vegan option
- Sautéed spinach or kale
- Cooked bacon or tempeh bacon for a vegan option
- Shredded cheddar cheese or dairy-free cheese for a vegan option
- Salsa or hot sauce (optional)
- Chopped chives or green onions for garnish
- Salt and pepper, to taste

Instructions:

1. Prepare the Gnocchi: Cook your sweet potato gnocchi as outlined in the classic sweet potato gnocchi recipe (Chapter 2) or your chosen variation.
2. Assemble the Bowl: In a bowl or on a plate, arrange the cooked sweet potato gnocchi, scrambled eggs or tofu scramble, sautéed spinach or kale, and cooked bacon or tempeh bacon.
3. Cheese and Garnish: Sprinkle shredded cheddar cheese or dairy-free cheese over the bowl. If you like some heat, add salsa or hot sauce. Garnish with chopped chives or green onions for a pop of freshness.
4. Season and Enjoy: Season your breakfast gnocchi bowl with salt and pepper to taste. This hearty and savory breakfast will leave you energized and ready to tackle the day.

These sweet potato gnocchi bowls offer a versatile way to enjoy this delightful dish for breakfast, lunch, or dinner. Customize the ingredients to suit your preferences and dietary needs, and savor the endless flavor possibilities.

Chapter 10: Sweet Potato Gnocchi Salads

In this chapter, we'll explore a lighter side of sweet potato gnocchi by incorporating them into vibrant and delicious salads. These salads are perfect for a refreshing meal or as a side dish that adds depth and flavor to any spread.

Roasted Veggie and Gnocchi Salad

Roasting vegetables and sweet potato gnocchi together creates a hearty and satisfying salad with a beautiful medley of flavors and textures.

Ingredients:

- 1 batch of sweet potato gnocchi (classic or your preferred variation)
- Assorted vegetables (bell peppers, cherry tomatoes, zucchini, red onion, etc.), cut into bite-sized pieces
- Olive oil
- Balsamic vinegar
- Fresh basil leaves, torn
- Feta cheese, crumbled (optional)
- Salt and pepper, to taste

Instructions:

1. Prepare the Gnocchi and Vegetables: Cook your sweet potato gnocchi as outlined in the classic sweet potato gnocchi recipe (Chapter 2) or your chosen variation. Toss the assorted vegetables in olive oil, salt, and pepper, then roast them in the oven until tender and slightly caramelized.

2. Combine and Dress: In a large bowl, combine the cooked sweet potato gnocchi and roasted vegetables. Drizzle with balsamic vinegar and toss to coat. Add fresh torn basil leaves and

crumbled feta cheese for extra flavor and texture.

3. Season and Serve: Season with additional salt and pepper if needed. Serve this roasted veggie and gnocchi salad warm or at room temperature for a delightful and hearty meal.

Caprese Gnocchi Salad

Capture the essence of a classic Caprese salad by pairing sweet potato gnocchi with fresh tomatoes, mozzarella cheese, and fragrant basil.

Ingredients:

- 1 batch of sweet potato gnocchi (classic or your preferred variation)
- Cherry tomatoes, halved
- Fresh mozzarella cheese, cubed
- Fresh basil leaves, torn
- Balsamic glaze
- Extra-virgin olive oil
- Salt and pepper, to taste

Instructions:

1. Prepare the Gnocchi: Cook your sweet potato gnocchi as outlined in the classic sweet potato gnocchi recipe (Chapter 2) or your chosen variation.
2. Assemble the Salad: In a bowl, combine the cooked sweet potato gnocchi, cherry tomato halves, fresh mozzarella cheese cubes, and torn basil leaves.

1. Dress and Garnish: Drizzle with balsamic glaze and extra-virgin olive oil for a burst of flavor. Season with salt and pepper to taste.
2. Serve: Enjoy this Caprese gnocchi salad as a refreshing and elegant dish that's perfect for any occasion.

Fruit and Nut Gnocchi Salad

This sweet and savory salad combines the rich flavors of sweet potato gnocchi with a medley of fruits, nuts, and a zesty dressing.

Ingredients:

- 1 batch of sweet potato gnocchi (classic or your preferred variation)
- Fresh mixed berries (strawberries, blueberries, raspberries, etc.)
- Fresh pineapple chunks
- Chopped nuts (walnuts, pecans, or almonds)
- Baby spinach or arugula
- Feta cheese, crumbled (optional)
- Balsamic vinaigrette dressing
- Salt and pepper, to taste

Instructions:

1. Prepare the Gnocchi: Cook your sweet potato gnocchi as outlined in the classic sweet potato gnocchi recipe (Chapter 2) or your chosen variation.
2. Assemble the Salad: In a large bowl, combine the cooked sweet potato gnocchi, fresh mixed berries, pineapple chunks, chopped nuts, and baby spinach or arugula.
3. Add Cheese: If desired, sprinkle crumbled feta cheese over the salad for an added layer of creaminess.
4. Dress and Season: Drizzle with balsamic vinaigrette dressing, and season with salt and pepper to taste.
5. Serve: Indulge in the delightful mix of flavors and textures in this fruit and nut gnocchi salad, which makes for a satisfying and refreshing meal.

These sweet potato gnocchi salads offer a delightful balance of flavors, making them perfect for light and enjoyable meals. Customize the ingredients to suit your preferences and celebrate the versatility of sweet potato gnocchi.

Chapter 11: Sweet Potato Gnocchi for the Holidays

In this chapter, we'll celebrate the joy of the holiday season by incorporating sweet potato gnocchi into special dishes that are perfect for Thanksgiving, Christmas, and New Year's Eve gatherings. These recipes will add a touch of warmth and comfort to your holiday feasts.

Thanksgiving Sweet Potato Gnocchi

Thanksgiving is a time to savor the flavors of fall. Incorporate sweet potato gnocchi into your holiday menu for a delightful twist on traditional dishes.

1. Sweet Potato Gnocchi with Sage Brown Butter and Cranberry Compote:

Ingredients: Sweet potato gnocchi, sage leaves, unsalted butter, cranberries, sugar, orange zest

Instructions: Sauté sweet potato gnocchi in sage-infused brown butter until golden and crisp. Serve with a cranberry compote, made by simmering cranberries, sugar, and orange zest until thickened. This dish combines the earthy warmth of sage with the sweet-tartness of cranberries, making it a Thanksgiving favorite.

2. Sweet Potato Gnocchi Stuffing:

Ingredients: Sweet potato gnocchi, cubed bread, celery, onions, sage, thyme, chicken or vegetable broth

Instructions: Create a unique stuffing by replacing traditional bread cubes with sweet potato gnocchi. Sauté celery, onions, and herbs, then mix them with the gnocchi and moisten with broth. Bake until golden brown for a flavorful and comforting side dish.

Christmas Gnocchi

Celebrate the magic of Christmas with sweet potato gnocchi recipes that embrace the holiday spirit.

1. Sweet Potato Gnocchi with Creamy Tomato and Spinach Sauce:

Ingredients: Sweet potato gnocchi, heavy cream, crushed tomatoes, spinach, Parmesan cheese, nutmeg

Instructions: Prepare sweet potato gnocchi and serve them in a creamy tomato sauce enriched with heavy cream, spinach, and Parmesan cheese. A touch of nutmeg adds a festive flair to this indulgent dish.

2. Roasted Vegetable and Sweet Potato Gnocchi Gratin:

Ingredients: Sweet potato gnocchi, roasted vegetables (carrots, Brussels sprouts, butternut squash), Gruyère cheese, breadcrumbs, fresh herbs

Instructions: Roast a medley of seasonal vegetables and combine them with sweet potato gnocchi in a gratin dish. Top with Gruyère cheese and breadcrumbs, then bake until golden and bubbly. This gratin is a delightful addition to your Christmas feast.

New Year's Eve Gnocchi

Ring in the New Year with elegant and celebratory sweet potato gnocchi dishes.

1. Champagne and Mushroom Sweet Potato Gnocchi:

Ingredients: Sweet potato gnocchi, Champagne, mixed mushrooms (such as chanterelles and shiitakes), shallots, heavy cream, fresh parsley

Instructions: Create a luxurious New Year's Eve dish by sautéing mixed mushrooms and shallots, then deglaze with Champagne and simmer with heavy cream. Toss sweet potato gnocchi in this decadent sauce and garnish with fresh parsley.

2. Lobster Bisque Gnocchi:

Ingredients: Sweet potato gnocchi, lobster bisque, cooked lobster meat, chives

Instructions: Elevate your New Year's celebration with lobster bisque-infused sweet potato gnocchi. Heat the bisque, add cooked lobster meat, and serve it over sweet potato gnocchi. Finish with a sprinkle of chives for an elegant touch.

These holiday-inspired sweet potato gnocchi recipes are perfect for creating memorable meals that capture the essence of Thanksgiving,

Christmas, and New Year's Eve. Share these dishes with loved ones to make your holiday gatherings extra special.

Chapter 12: Sweet Potato Gnocchi for Lunch

In this chapter, we'll explore the versatility of sweet potato gnocchi as a delicious and satisfying option for lunchtime. Whether you're looking for portable lunch ideas, office-friendly gnocchi dishes, or quick and easy recipes, you'll find delightful options to enjoy during your midday break.

Portable Lunch Ideas

For those on the go, these portable sweet potato gnocchi dishes are easy to pack and enjoy wherever your lunchtime takes you.

1. Sweet Potato Gnocchi Salad Jars:

Ingredients: Sweet potato gnocchi, mixed greens, cherry tomatoes, cucumbers, bell peppers, vinaigrette dressing

Instructions: Cook sweet potato gnocchi and let them cool. Layer them with mixed greens, cherry tomatoes, cucumbers, and bell peppers in a mason jar. Drizzle with your favorite vinaigrette dressing for a portable and refreshing salad.

2. Sweet Potato Gnocchi Wraps:

Ingredients: Sweet potato gnocchi, tortillas, hummus, roasted red peppers, spinach, feta cheese

Instructions: Cook sweet potato gnocchi, then place them on a tortilla. Add hummus, roasted red peppers, spinach, and crumbled feta cheese. Roll up the tortilla and enjoy a flavorful gnocchi wrap.

Office-Friendly Gnocchi

When you need a satisfying lunch at the office, these sweet potato gnocchi dishes can be prepared ahead of time and reheated for a delicious meal.

1. Sweet Potato Gnocchi with Spinach and Creamy Tomato Sauce:

Ingredients: Sweet potato gnocchi, spinach, creamy tomato sauce (prepared in advance)

Instructions: Cook sweet potato gnocchi, sauté spinach, and reheat the creamy tomato sauce. Combine them for a hearty and office-friendly lunch.

2. Sweet Potato Gnocchi Stir-Fry:

Ingredients: Sweet potato gnocchi, mixed vegetables (bell peppers, broccoli, snap peas), teriyaki sauce

Instructions: Cook sweet potato gnocchi and set them aside. In a pan, stir-fry mixed vegetables until tender, then add the cooked gnocchi and teriyaki sauce for a flavorful lunch option.

Quick and Easy Recipes

For busy days when you need a quick and satisfying lunch, these sweet potato gnocchi recipes come together in no time.

1. Garlic and Herb Sweet Potato Gnocchi:

Ingredients: Sweet potato gnocchi, butter, minced garlic, fresh herbs (such as rosemary and thyme), grated Parmesan cheese

Instructions: Cook sweet potato gnocchi, then toss them in a pan with melted butter, minced garlic, and fresh herbs. Finish with grated Parmesan cheese for a simple yet flavorful lunch.

2. Sweet Potato Gnocchi with Pesto and Cherry Tomatoes:

Ingredients: Sweet potato gnocchi, pesto sauce (store-bought or homemade), cherry tomatoes, fresh basil leaves

Instructions: Cook sweet potato gnocchi, then toss them with pesto sauce and halved cherry tomatoes. Garnish with fresh basil leaves for a quick and vibrant lunch.

These sweet potato gnocchi lunch ideas are designed to fit your busy schedule while still delivering delicious and satisfying meals. Whether you're at the office or on the go, these recipes make lunchtime a delightful experience.

Chapter 13: Sweet Potato Gnocchi Sides

In this chapter, we'll explore the versatility of sweet potato gnocchi as a delightful addition to your side dish repertoire. Whether you're looking for complementary gnocchi and veggie side dishes, gnocchi with dips and spreads, or creative gnocchi-stuffed veggies, you'll find plenty of options to elevate your meals.

Gnocchi and Veggie Side Dishes

Enhance your main courses with these flavorful sweet potato gnocchi and veggie side dishes.

1. Sautéed Sweet Potato Gnocchi with Garlic and Spinach:

Ingredients: Sweet potato gnocchi, garlic, fresh spinach, olive oil, Parmesan cheese

Instructions: Sauté sweet potato gnocchi in olive oil until lightly browned. Add minced garlic and fresh spinach, and continue cooking until the spinach wilts. Top with grated Parmesan cheese for a simple and savory side dish.

2. Roasted Sweet Potato Gnocchi with Brussels Sprouts and Balsamic Glaze:

Ingredients: Sweet potato gnocchi, Brussels sprouts, olive oil, balsamic glaze, crushed red pepper flakes

Instructions: Toss sweet potato gnocchi and halved Brussels sprouts in olive oil, season with salt and pepper, and roast until caramelized. Drizzle with balsamic glaze and a pinch of crushed red pepper flakes for a flavorful side.

Gnocchi with Dips and Spreads

Turn sweet potato gnocchi into the perfect vehicle for delicious dips and spreads.

1. Sweet Potato Gnocchi with Whipped Goat Cheese and Honey:

Ingredients: Sweet potato gnocchi, goat cheese, honey, fresh rosemary

Instructions: Cook sweet potato gnocchi and serve them with a side of whipped goat cheese. Drizzle with honey and garnish with fresh rosemary for a sweet and tangy appetizer or side dish.

2. Gnocchi with Roasted Red Pepper Hummus:

Ingredients: Sweet potato gnocchi, roasted red pepper hummus, fresh parsley

Instructions: Cook sweet potato gnocchi and serve with a bowl of roasted red pepper hummus. Garnish with fresh parsley for a flavorful and creamy dip.

Gnocchi-Stuffed Veggies

Get creative by using sweet potato gnocchi to stuff your favorite vegetables.

1. Stuffed Bell Peppers with Sweet Potato Gnocchi and Sausage:

Ingredients: Sweet potato gnocchi, bell peppers, cooked sausage, marinara sauce, mozzarella cheese

Instructions: Cut the tops off bell peppers, remove the seeds, and stuff them with cooked sweet potato gnocchi, cooked sausage, marinara sauce, and mozzarella cheese. Bake until the peppers are tender and the filling is hot and bubbly.

2. Gnocchi-Stuffed Mushrooms with Garlic Butter:

Ingredients: Sweet potato gnocchi, large mushroom caps, garlic butter, fresh parsley

Instructions: Cook sweet potato gnocchi and stuff them into large mushroom caps.

Drizzle with garlic butter and bake until the mushrooms are tender. Garnish with fresh parsley for an elegant side dish.

These sweet potato gnocchi side dishes add a burst of flavor and creativity to your meals. Whether you're serving them alongside a main course or as appetizers, they are sure to delight your taste buds and impress your guests.

Chapter 14: International Sweet Potato Gnocchi

In this chapter, we embark on a culinary journey exploring sweet potato gnocchi from around the world. Discover global flavors and inspirations that bring new dimensions to this beloved dish, as well as creative fusion gnocchi recipes that blend elements from different cuisines.

Sweet Potato Gnocchi from Around the World

Explore traditional sweet potato gnocchi recipes from various countries and regions.

1. Japanese Sweet Potato Gnocchi (Satsumaimo Gnocchi):

Ingredients: Japanese satsumaimo sweet potatoes, potato starch, soy sauce, sesame seeds

Instructions: Create satsumaimo sweet potato gnocchi by mixing mashed satsumaimo sweet potatoes with potato starch. Cook them until they float, then serve with a drizzle of soy sauce and a sprinkle of sesame seeds for a delightful Japanese twist.

2. Argentine Sweet Potato Gnocchi (Ñoquis de Batata):

Ingredients: Sweet potatoes, flour, salt

Instructions: Combine mashed sweet potatoes with flour and a pinch of salt to make ñoquis de batata. These Argentine sweet potato gnocchi are traditionally enjoyed on the 29th of each month for good luck. Serve with your favorite sauce.

Global Flavors and Inspirations

Discover sweet potato gnocchi recipes inspired by the diverse cuisines of the world.

1. Indian Sweet Potato Gnocchi with Spiced Tomato Curry:

Ingredients: Sweet potato gnocchi, tomato-based curry sauce, Indian spices (such as cumin, coriander, and turmeric), fresh cilantro

Instructions: Cook sweet potato gnocchi and serve them in a spiced tomato curry sauce infused with Indian flavors. Garnish with fresh cilantro for a mouthwatering fusion dish.

2. Thai-Inspired Sweet Potato Gnocchi with Coconut and Lemongrass:

Ingredients: Sweet potato gnocchi, coconut milk, lemongrass, Thai curry paste, fresh basil leaves

Instructions: Prepare sweet potato gnocchi and serve them in a creamy coconut and lemongrass sauce inspired by Thai cuisine. Add Thai curry paste for a kick of flavor and garnish with fresh basil leaves.

Fusion Gnocchi

Experience the delightful fusion of flavors with creative sweet potato gnocchi recipes.

1. Mexican Sweet Potato Gnocchi with Chipotle Cream Sauce:

Ingredients: Sweet potato gnocchi, chipotle cream sauce, black beans, corn, fresh cilantro, queso fresco

Instructions: Cook sweet potato gnocchi and serve them with a smoky chipotle cream sauce. Top with black beans, corn, fresh cilantro, and crumbled queso fresco for a fusion of Mexican and Italian flavors.

2. Mediterranean-Mexican Fusion Gnocchi:

Ingredients: Sweet potato gnocchi, Mediterranean-inspired tomato sauce, chorizo, olives, feta cheese, fresh parsley

Instructions: Prepare sweet potato gnocchi and serve them with a Mediterranean-inspired tomato sauce. Add cooked chorizo, olives, crumbled feta cheese, and fresh parsley for a fusion twist that combines the best of both cuisines.

These international sweet potato gnocchi recipes showcase the incredible diversity of flavors and inspirations from around the world. Whether you're craving traditional dishes or inventive fusion creations, these recipes will transport your taste buds on a global adventure.

Chapter 15: Sweet Potato Gnocchi Desserts

In this delightful chapter, we'll explore the sweet side of sweet potato gnocchi. Transform this beloved dish into a delicious dessert with a variety of creative recipes, decadent dessert sauces and toppings, and indulgent gnocchi-based sweet treats.

Sweet Potato Gnocchi as a Sweet Treat

Discover how sweet potato gnocchi can be the star of your dessert table.

1. Sweet Potato Gnocchi with Cinnamon Sugar and Vanilla Ice Cream:

Ingredients: Sweet potato gnocchi, cinnamon sugar, vanilla ice cream, caramel sauce

Instructions: Prepare sweet potato gnocchi and toss them in cinnamon sugar. Serve them warm over a scoop of vanilla ice cream and drizzle with caramel sauce for a simple yet delightful dessert.

2. Sweet Potato Gnocchi with Chocolate Ganache and Berries:

Ingredients: Sweet potato gnocchi, chocolate ganache, fresh berries (strawberries, raspberries, blueberries), powdered sugar

Instructions: Cook sweet potato gnocchi and drizzle them with rich chocolate ganache. Top with a medley of fresh berries and a dusting of powdered sugar for an elegant dessert.

Dessert Sauces and Toppings

Elevate your sweet potato gnocchi desserts with decadent sauces and toppings.

1. Salted Caramel Sauce:

Ingredients: Sugar, butter, heavy cream, sea salt

Instructions: Make a luscious salted caramel sauce by melting sugar, adding butter and heavy cream, and seasoning with sea salt. Drizzle over sweet potato gnocchi desserts for a sweet and savory contrast.

2. Raspberry Coulis:

Ingredients: Fresh or frozen raspberries, sugar, lemon juice

Instructions: Create a vibrant raspberry coulis by blending raspberries with sugar and lemon juice. Strain to remove seeds, and use it as a fruity topping for your dessert gnocchi.

Creative Dessert Gnocchi Recipes

Experience the joy of crafting unique and indulgent dessert gnocchi recipes.

1. Sweet Potato Gnocchi S'mores:

Ingredients: Sweet potato gnocchi, marshmallows, chocolate chips, graham cracker crumbs

Instructions: Cook sweet potato gnocchi, then skewer them with marshmallows and roast until golden. Sprinkle with chocolate chips and graham cracker crumbs for a delectable s'mores-inspired treat.

2. Caramel Apple Stuffed Gnocchi:

Ingredients: Sweet potato gnocchi, caramel sauce, apple compote, chopped pecans

Instructions: Prepare sweet potato gnocchi and stuff them with a mixture of caramel sauce, apple compote, and chopped pecans. Serve as a warm and comforting dessert.

These sweet potato gnocchi dessert recipes prove that gnocchi can shine as a sweet treat. Whether you're craving a simple yet satisfying dessert or an indulgent creation, these recipes will satisfy your sweet tooth and add a touch of elegance to any occasion.

Chapter 16: Gluten-Free and Vegan Options

In this chapter, we'll cater to dietary preferences and restrictions by exploring gluten-free sweet potato gnocchi, vegan gnocchi recipes, and tips for substituting ingredients to accommodate a gluten-free and vegan lifestyle.

Gluten-Free Sweet Potato Gnocchi

Enjoy the deliciousness of sweet potato gnocchi without gluten.

1. Classic Gluten-Free Sweet Potato Gnocchi:

Ingredients: Sweet potatoes, gluten-free flour blend, salt

Instructions: Create gluten-free sweet potato gnocchi by using a gluten-free flour blend in place of traditional wheat flour. Follow the classic gnocchi recipe (Chapter 2) for guidance on making gluten-free gnocchi.

2. Gluten-Free Spinach and Sweet Potato Gnocchi:

Ingredients: Sweet potatoes, spinach, gluten-free flour blend, salt

Instructions: Make gluten-free spinach and sweet potato gnocchi by incorporating fresh spinach into the dough along with a gluten-free flour blend. Follow the basic steps of the classic gnocchi recipe (Chapter 2) for guidance.

Vegan Gnocchi Recipes

Discover vegan sweet potato gnocchi recipes that omit animal products.

1. Vegan Sweet Potato Gnocchi with Vegan Pesto:

Ingredients: Sweet potato gnocchi (made with vegan substitutions), vegan pesto sauce, cherry tomatoes, pine nuts, fresh basil leaves

Instructions: Prepare vegan sweet potato gnocchi by using plant-based alternatives for eggs and cheese in the classic gnocchi recipe (Chapter 2). Serve with vegan pesto, cherry tomatoes, pine nuts, and fresh basil leaves for a delightful vegan meal.

2. Vegan Butternut Squash and Sweet Potato Gnocchi:

Ingredients: Sweet potatoes, butternut squash, gluten-free flour blend (or regular flour), nutritional yeast (for cheesy flavor), salt

Instructions: Make vegan butternut squash and sweet potato gnocchi by blending sweet potatoes and butternut squash for the base. Use a gluten-free flour blend for a gluten-free version, and nutritional yeast for added cheesy flavor. Follow the classic gnocchi recipe (Chapter 2) with these substitutions.

Substituting Ingredients

Learn how to substitute ingredients to create gluten-free and vegan sweet potato gnocchi.

1. Egg Substitutes:

Replace eggs with flax eggs (1 tablespoon ground flaxseed mixed with 2.5 tablespoons water per egg) or applesauce (1/4 cup per egg) for vegan gnocchi.

2. Cheese Substitutes:

Use dairy-free cheese alternatives or nutritional yeast for a cheesy flavor in vegan gnocchi recipes.

3. Flour Substitutes:

opt for gluten-free flour blends made from rice, potato, or almond flour for gluten-free gnocchi.

4. Milk Substitutes:

Replace dairy milk with almond milk, soy milk, or any preferred plant-based milk in vegan gnocchi recipes.

5. Butter Substitutes:

Substitute dairy butter with vegan butter or coconut oil for vegan recipes.

By making thoughtful ingredient substitutions and following these recipes, you can create delicious gluten-free and vegan sweet potato gnocchi dishes that cater to various dietary needs while preserving the flavors and textures you love.

Chapter 17: Homemade Sweet Potato Gnocchi vs. Store-Bought

In this chapter, we'll explore the advantages and disadvantages of making homemade sweet potato gnocchi versus using store-bought options. We'll also provide guidance on selecting high-quality store-bought gnocchi and conduct a taste test to compare the two.

Pros and Cons

Let's begin by examining the pros and cons of both homemade and store-bought sweet potato gnocchi.

Homemade Sweet Potato Gnocchi:

Pros:

Freshness: Homemade gnocchi are made from scratch with fresh ingredients, resulting in a delightful taste and texture.

Customization: You have full control over the ingredients, allowing you to cater to dietary preferences and flavor profiles.

Satisfaction: The process of making gnocchi from scratch can be a rewarding culinary experience.

Cons:

Time-Consuming: Preparing homemade gnocchi can be time-consuming, requiring careful preparation and shaping.

Skill Level: Gnocchi-making may require practice to achieve the perfect texture and consistency.

Ingredient Availability: Some ingredients for homemade gnocchi may not be readily available.

Store-Bought Sweet Potato Gnocchi:

Pros:

Convenience: Store-bought gnocchi are quick and easy to prepare, making them a time-saving option for busy cooks.

Consistency: High-quality store-bought gnocchi offer a consistent taste and texture.

Variety: You can find a variety of flavors and types of store-bought gnocchi to suit your preferences.

Cons:

Preservatives: Some store-bought gnocchi may contain preservatives or additives.

Less Customization: You have limited control over the ingredients and flavor when using pre-made gnocchi.

How to Choose Quality Store-Bought Gnocchi

If you opt for store-bought sweet potato gnocchi, here are some tips on selecting quality options:

Read the Label: Check the ingredient list for minimal additives and preservatives. Look for gnocchi made with real sweet potatoes.

Texture: High-quality gnocchi should have a firm but tender texture. Avoid packages with gnocchi that feel mushy or overly soft.

Brand Reputation: Research reputable brands known for their quality pasta products.

Flavor Variations: Explore different flavor variations, such as classic, spinach, or butternut squash, to find your favorite.

Fresh vs. Frozen: Some stores offer fresh, refrigerated gnocchi, while others sell frozen options. Choose based on your preference and convenience.

Taste Test and Comparison

To determine which option is right for you, consider conducting a taste test and comparison. Prepare homemade sweet potato gnocchi using your favorite recipe and a high-quality store-bought variety. Here's how:

Cook both homemade and store-bought gnocchi according to their respective instructions.

Taste Test: Evaluate the flavor, texture, and overall quality of each type of gnocchi. Pay attention to factors like freshness, tenderness, and how well they hold sauce.

Consider Convenience: Think about the time and effort required for each option. Is the convenience of store-bought worth it, or do you prefer the satisfaction of making gnocchi from scratch?

Ultimately, whether you choose homemade or store-bought sweet potato gnocchi depends on your preferences, available time, and desired level of customization. Both options can yield delicious results, and it's a matter of finding what works best for you.

Chapter 18: Tips and Troubleshooting

In this chapter, we'll delve into the world of sweet potato gnocchi with a focus on tips and troubleshooting. You'll learn how to avoid common gnocchi-making mistakes, troubleshoot issues that may arise during the process, and discover expert tips for crafting perfect gnocchi every time.

Common Gnocchi-Making Mistakes

Let's start by addressing some of the most common mistakes when making sweet potato gnocchi.

Overworking the Dough: Kneading or mixing the dough too much can lead to tough gnocchi. Mix until just combined to maintain a tender texture.

Using the Wrong Potatoes: Choose sweet potatoes that are dry and starchy, as watery sweet potatoes can result in a wet dough. Avoid using overly fibrous sweet potatoes.

Adding Too Much Flour: Using excessive flour can make gnocchi heavy and dense. Add flour gradually until the dough reaches the desired consistency.

Skipping the Potato Ricer: Ensure your sweet potatoes are properly riced to avoid lumps and achieve a smooth dough. A potato ricer or food mill is essential.

Not Dusting with Flour: To prevent sticking, lightly dust your work surface and gnocchi with flour during the shaping process.

Troubleshooting Guide

Encounter an issue while making sweet potato gnocchi? Use this troubleshooting guide to help you resolve common problems.

Gnocchi are Too Dense:

Solution: Overworking the dough or adding too much flour can lead to dense gnocchi. Start with a lighter hand when mixing and adding flour gradually.

Gnocchi Fall Apart During Cooking:

Solution: This can occur if the dough is too wet or if the gnocchi are overcooked. Ensure your sweet potatoes are dry and starchy, and cook the gnocchi until they float to the surface.

Gnocchi Stick Together:

Solution: Gnocchi may stick if they are placed too close together while resting. Ensure they are spaced apart and lightly dusted with flour.

Gnocchi Are Irregular in Size:

Solution: Consistency in size ensures even cooking. Use a gnocchi board or fork to create uniform shapes.

Gnocchi Have a Gummy Texture:

Solution: Overcooking can result in a gummy texture. Cook until the gnocchi float to the surface and remove them promptly.

Expert Tips for Perfect Gnocchi

Achieve gnocchi perfection with these expert tips:

Choose the Right Sweet Potatoes: Select dry, starchy sweet potatoes with orange flesh for the best results.

Use a Potato Ricer: Invest in a potato ricer or food mill to achieve consistently smooth sweet potato puree.

Work on a Lightly Floured Surface: Keep your work surface and hands lightly floured to prevent sticking.

Test a Few Gnocchi First: Cook a small batch of gnocchi as a test to ensure the dough and cooking time are correct before proceeding with the full batch.

Experiment with Flavors: Don't hesitate to experiment with different seasonings, herbs, and sauces to create unique sweet potato gnocchi dishes.

With these tips and troubleshooting guidance, you'll be well-prepared to tackle sweet potato gnocchi-making with confidence. Overcome challenges and savor the satisfaction of creating perfect gnocchi each time.

Chapter 19: Sweet Potato Gnocchi for Beginners

In this chapter, we'll guide beginners through the process of making sweet potato gnocchi step-by-step. You'll learn the fundamentals of gnocchi-making, build confidence in your skills, and explore basic recipes and variations to get you started on your culinary journey.

Step-by-Step for Novices

Let's start by breaking down the gnocchi-making process into simple steps for beginners:

Choose the Right Sweet Potatoes: Select dry, starchy sweet potatoes with orange flesh. Bake or boil them until tender and easy to mash.

Prepare the Sweet Potato Puree: Peel the cooked sweet potatoes and use a potato ricer or food mill to create a smooth puree.

Mix with Flour and Salt: Combine the sweet potato puree with all-purpose flour and a pinch of salt. Mix until just combined to form a dough.

Shape the Gnocchi: Divide the dough into smaller portions and roll them into ropes. Cut the ropes into bite-sized pieces. Use a gnocchi board or fork to create ridges on the gnocchi.

Boil the Gnocchi: Bring a pot of salted water to a boil and gently drop in the gnocchi. Cook until they float to the surface, indicating they are done.

Sauté or Serve: You can sauté the cooked gnocchi in a pan with butter or your favorite sauce for added flavor, or simply serve them with your preferred sauce.

Building Confidence in Gnocchi-Making

Gnocchi-making is an art that improves with practice. Here are some tips to help you build confidence:

Start with Basic Recipes: Begin with basic sweet potato gnocchi recipes that use a minimal number of ingredients.

Practice Shaping Techniques: Shaping gnocchi can be challenging at first. Practice rolling and shaping until you feel comfortable.

Experiment with Variations: Gradually explore variations by incorporating different flavors, herbs, and sauces into your recipes.

Take Notes: Keep a notebook to jot down your experiences, including what worked well and what you'd like to improve.

Embrace Imperfections: Gnocchi don't have to be perfect; they should be made with love and enjoyed with enthusiasm.

Basic Recipes and Variations

To get you started, here are two basic sweet potato gnocchi recipes along with variations:

1. Classic Sweet Potato Gnocchi:

Ingredients: Sweet potatoes, all-purpose flour, salt

Instructions: Follow the step-by-step process outlined earlier for classic sweet potato gnocchi. Serve with your favorite sauce.

2. Spinach and Sweet Potato Gnocchi:

Ingredients: Sweet potatoes, fresh spinach, all-purpose flour, salt

Instructions: Incorporate finely chopped fresh spinach into the sweet potato dough. Follow the same steps for shaping and cooking as in the classic recipe. Serve with a light butter and sage sauce.

As a beginner, start with these recipes and gradually explore variations as you gain confidence in your gnocchi-making skills. With practice and a sense of adventure, you'll become a sweet potato gnocchi expert in no time!

Chapter 20: Sweet Potato Gnocchi for Seasoned Cooks

In this chapter, we'll elevate sweet potato gnocchi-making to an advanced level. Seasoned cooks can explore advanced techniques, push the boundaries of flavor, and create chef-inspired sweet potato gnocchi creations that are sure to impress.

Advanced Techniques

Let's begin by delving into advanced techniques that will take your sweet potato gnocchi to the next level:

Herb-Infused Gnocchi: Experiment with herb-infused sweet potato gnocchi by incorporating finely chopped fresh herbs like rosemary, thyme, or sage into the dough. This adds a burst of flavor.

Colored Gnocchi: Create visually stunning gnocchi by incorporating natural colorants like beetroot or spinach puree into the dough. This adds vibrancy to your dishes.

Gnocchi Stamps: Invest in gnocchi stamps or specialty gnocchi boards to create unique shapes and textures for your gnocchi. These tools add elegance to your dishes.

Advanced Sauces: Pair your sweet potato gnocchi with complex, chef-worthy sauces like truffle cream sauce, saffron-infused beurre blanc, or a rich duck ragù.

Pushing the Boundaries of Flavor

Now, let's explore how to push the boundaries of flavor in sweet potato gnocchi:

Fusion Flavors: Combine elements from different cuisines to create fusion sweet potato gnocchi dishes. For example, blend Italian gnocchi with Asian-inspired flavors like miso butter or ginger soy sauce.

Infused Oils: Experiment with infused oils like garlic-infused olive oil or chili-infused sesame oil to drizzle over your gnocchi for an extra layer of flavor.

Creative Fillings: Take inspiration from dumpling-making techniques and create stuffed sweet potato gnocchi with fillings like goat cheese and roasted garlic, or braised short rib.

Homemade Garnishes: Elevate your dishes with homemade garnishes like crispy prosciutto chips, candied nuts, or microgreens.

Chef-Inspired Creations

Challenge yourself to create chef-inspired sweet potato gnocchi dishes:

Lobster and Sweet Potato Gnocchi with Champagne Cream Sauce: Craft a luxurious dish by pairing sweet potato gnocchi with lobster tail and a decadent champagne cream sauce.

Truffle and Mushroom Sweet Potato Gnocchi Risotto: Create a gourmet experience by incorporating truffle oil, wild mushrooms, and a creamy risotto-style sauce.

Blue Cheese and Walnut Sweet Potato Gnocchi with Poached Pears: Elevate your gnocchi with a combination of blue cheese, toasted walnuts, and poached pears for a harmonious blend of flavors and textures.

Foie Gras-Stuffed Sweet Potato Gnocchi: Push the boundaries of indulgence by crafting sweet potato gnocchi with a foie gras filling and a port wine reduction sauce.

As a seasoned cook, you have the skills and creativity to experiment with advanced techniques and flavors in your sweet potato gnocchi creations. These chef-inspired ideas provide a starting point for you to craft gourmet dishes that are sure to dazzle the palate.

Congratulations on embarking on a delightful journey into the world of sweet potato gnocchi! Throughout this cookbook, we've explored the art of crafting these delectable, pillowy bites of goodness. Whether you're a novice in the kitchen or a seasoned cook, there's a sweet potato gnocchi recipe here to suit your culinary desires.

From the very basics of choosing the right sweet potatoes and kneading your dough to perfection, to advanced techniques that push the boundaries of flavor, we've covered it all. You've learned how to create classic sweet potato gnocchi, explored a world of flavor variations, and even ventured into the realm of sweet potato gnocchi desserts.

Whether you're savoring them in a simple brown butter and sage sauce or creating gourmet masterpieces that would make a chef proud, sweet potato gnocchi are a versatile canvas for your culinary creativity.

Remember, the heart of cooking lies not just in the ingredients and techniques but in the joy it brings to your table. Share your sweet potato gnocchi creations with loved ones, savor the smiles around your dining table, and let the aromas and flavors transport you to a world of culinary delight.

As you continue your culinary adventures, don't hesitate to experiment, innovate, and make these sweet potato gnocchi recipes your own. The possibilities are endless, and the journey is as rewarding as the destination.

So, roll up your sleeves, tie on your apron, and let the enchanting aroma of sweet potato gnocchi fill your kitchen. It's time to indulge in the magic of homemade gnocchi and create memorable meals that will linger in your heart and on your taste buds for years to come.

Happy cooking, and may your sweet potato gnocchi always be a source of comfort, creativity, and culinary joy!

Bon appétit!